All About Food Crops

BANANAS

Cecelia H. Brannon

Enslow Publishing
101 W. 23rd Street
Suite 240
New York, NY 10011
USA

enslow.com

Published in 2018 by Enslow Publishing, LLC
101 W. 23rd Street, Suite 240 New York, NY 10011

Library of Congress Cataloguing-in-Publication Data

Names: Brannon, Cecelia H., author. | Brannon, Cecelia H. All about food crops.
Title: Bananas / Cecelia H. Brannon.
Description: New York, NY : Enslow Publishing, 2018. | Series: All about food crops | Audience: Pre-K to grade 1. | Includes bibliographical references and index.
Identifiers: LCCN 2017002020| ISBN 9780766085770 (library-bound) | ISBN 9780766088290 (pbk.) | ISBN 9780766088238 (6-pack)
Subjects: LCSH: Bananas—Juvenile literature.
Classification: LCC SB379.B2 B69 2018 | DDC 634/.772—dc23
LC record available at https://lccn.loc.gov/2017002020

Printed in the United States of America

To Our Readers: We have done our best to make sure all websites in this book were active and appropriate when we went to press. However, the author and the publisher have no control over and assume no liability for the material available on those websites or on any websites they may link to. Any comments or suggestions can be sent by email to customerservice@enslow.com.

Photo Credits: Cover, p. 1 Anna Jedynak/Shutterdsock.com; pp. 3 (left), 16 PhumjaiFcNightsky/Shutterstock.com; pp. 3 (center), 10 Salvador Aznar/Shutterstock.com; pp. 3 (right), 18 Jelena Yukka/Shutterstock.com; pp. 4-5 Kylie Walls/Shutterstock.com; p. 6 paulrommer/Shutterstock.com; p. 8 T.W. van Urk/Shutterstock.com; p. 12 tclound/Shutterstock.com; p. 14 MIA Studio/Shutterstock.com; p. 20 Chad Zuber/Shutterstock.com; p. 22 KidStock/Blend Images/Getty Images.

Contents

Words to Know

hand   herb   ripen

Bananas are an important crop.

Bananas are one of the most popular fruits in the world. More than 100 billion are eaten every year!

Bananas are grown in more than 100 countries. Banana plants need to live in very hot weather.

Bananas don't grow on trees. They grow on the world's largest herb! A tree has a woody trunk. An herb does not.

A banana plant can grow to be 25 feet (8 meters) high!

Bananas are usually picked while they are still green. Bananas ripen, or become ready to eat, when they turn yellow.

Bananas grow in large hanging bunches called **hands**.

The most common kind of banana has a yellow peel. But bananas also come in other colors, like red.

In many tropical places, people wrap food in the leaves and then cook it. Tamales are a popular dish.

Bananas are just as good for you as they are tasty!

Read More

Gibbons, Gail. *The Fruits We Eat*. New York, NY: Holiday House, 2015.

Hansen, Grace. *Fruit*. North Mankato, MN: Abdo Kids, 2016.

Rattini, Kristin Baird. *National Geographic Readers: Seed to Plant*. Wasington, DC: National Geographic, 2014.

Websites

Kids Cooking Activities
www.kids-cooking-activities.com/banana-facts.html
Check out some easy banana recipes to try with an adult.

Science Kids
www.sciencekids.co.nz/sciencefacts/food/bananas.html
Learn more facts about bananas.

Index

Guided Reading Level: C
Guided Reading Leveling System is based on the guidelines recommended by Fountas and Pinnell.

Word Count: 149